HOW TO RUN FACEBOOK ADVERTISING FOR YOUR MOBILE APP GAME IN 2019

A PRIMER

MICHAEL B. CASTILLE

Copyright © 2019 by Michael B. Castille

All rights reserved.

No part of this book may be reproduced in any form or by any electronic or mechanical means, including information storage and retrieval systems, without written permission from the author, except for the use of brief quotations in a book review.

You have brains in your head. You have feet in your shoes. You can steer yourself any direction you choose.

— DR. SEUSS

CONTENTS

PART I. BEFORE YOU LAUNCH ON FACEBOOK
1. Introduction — 3
2. When to Use Facebook — 4
3. Planning — 7
4. Technical Setup — 10

PART II. SETTING UP FACEBOOK
5. Audience Setup — 15
6. Campaign Setup — 25
7. Ad Set Setup — 31
8. Ad Setup — 43

PART III. CAMPAIGN MANAGEMENT
9. Column Setup — 53
10. Daily Management — 55
11. Benchmarks — 58
12. Weekly Management — 61

PART IV. TIPS AND TRICKS
13. Best Practices — 67
14. Cool Features — 73

Conclusion — 81
Appendix I: Additional Resources — 83
Appendix II: Terms — 87

PART I. BEFORE YOU LAUNCH ON FACEBOOK

INTRODUCTION

This book gives you the big picture, and a fist full of weeds, regarding how to run Facebook advertising for your mobile gaming app. As long as you have technical smarts, and preferably some marketing experience under your belt, then this should be a great, little primer. For all the gaps I leave - after all, this is a ***primer*** - then the Internet is your best friend.

A word of caution: my background is in mobile gaming (as in Angry Birds, Clash Royale, etc., not casino-type gaming). For non-gaming apps, much of this book should apply, but much of it may not. I'll point these issues out as we go along.

2

WHEN TO USE FACEBOOK

Before you even think about running user acquisition on Facebook, you need to have two things: a **good app** and a **need**. Below, I'll discuss how to know if your app is good, and how to know if you have a need:

DO YOU HAVE A GOOD APP?

If your app is horrible, then you should not waste money on Facebook, because you can't buy your way to success. So how can you tell if your app is good?

Retention: Retention is a metric that indicates how long a particular cohort continues to use your app. Let's say that in the month of June (which is a "cohort"), you acquire 10,000 users. You'll track these June users over time to see how long they stayed with you. You need at least a 30% day-1 retention to know that you have something. You won't get much more than 40 or 50% so don't kill yourself. Day 7 retention needs to be about 15% and day 30 about 6 or 7%. You'll use a tool like AppsFlyer to measure this, which we'll talk about in the

"Technical Setup" chapter. If your retention is poor, then have your developers fix the app until retention is healthy. See the chart below for a reference.

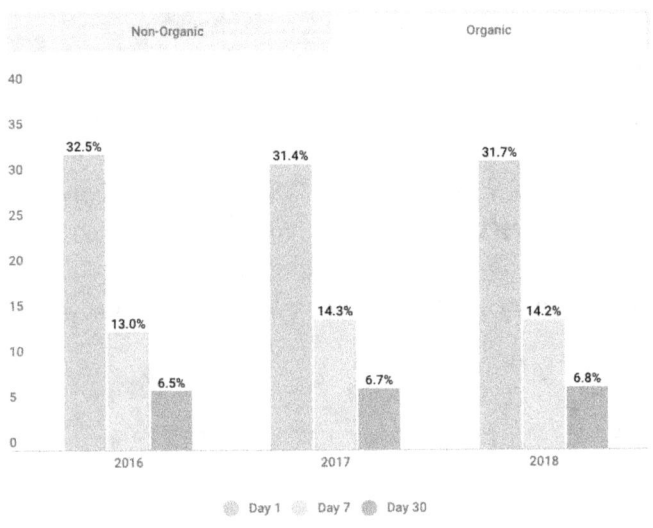

Source: AppsFlyer https://www.appsflyer.com/resources/2018-retention-benchmarks/

Monetization: Great, so your retention is healthy. But that still doesn't mean your app is any good. The next metric to consider is monetization. Monetization simply means how much users are spending in your app. In the world of app marketing, we measure this by "ARPU" or (average revenue per user) and "ROAS" (return on ad spend). For organic users, we only look at ARPU, since there is no ad spend by which to calculate a ROAS. Unlike the retention metrics above, there's a huge variability in ARPU healthiness. It all depends on your game genre, the geographies the users live in and the OS (hint: iOS monetizes much better than Android, generally speaking). When looking at only United States, check that your ARPU after day 1 is at least $0.07. Ideally, more like $0.20. Don't consider the ARPUs of countries like Brazil, India, Russia, and China. Those geos don't typically monetize anyway, and even if they did, it's in no way an indicator that your game will be a success. You need your game to work in the US, so check that geo's monetization.

In conclusion, if you are able to keep users interested in your app (i.e. healthy retention) and they're spending money in your app (i.e. monetization) then you have a **good app**. If you're not, then keep developing your app until it's good. This is what soft launches help you measure. Do an internet search to understand this in more detail, as it's outside the scope of this book.

DO YOU NEED TO SPEND MONEY ON ADVERTISING?

Organic performance: In general, we only want to think about spending money on Facebook, or any other paid network for that matter, when and if organic revenue can't support your business objectives. After all, if you're raking in tons of money organically, then why spend money on UA? With that said, most apps do need paid user acquisition to support their business objectives.

3

PLANNING

Before you create your ads, there are a few things you need to do first, one of them being planning.

PLAN YOUR AUDIENCES AND BUDGET ALLOCATION

Normally, a good old-fashioned spreadsheet will help you in your planning. Below is a screenshot of a typical Facebook Plan that I use, and you should create something similar.

PURCH FUNNEL	ANDROID OR IOS	GEO	TYPE	GENDER	AGE	FB INTEREST	BUDGET
BROAD	IOS	TIER 2	AEO	MF	18-55	LAL PURCH	$250
BROAD	IOS	TIER 3	AEO	MF	18-55	LAL PURCH	$250
BROAD	IOS	TIER 1	AEO	MF	18-55	LAL PURCH	$250
BROAD	AND	TIER 1	AI	MF	18-55	GAMER	$400
BROAD	AND	TIER 2	AI	MF	18-55	GAMER	$400
BROAD	AND	TIER 3	AI	MF	18-55	GAMER	$400
MID-VALUE	IOS	TIER 1	AEO	M	18-55	LAL PURCH	$250
MID-VALUE	IOS	TIER 2	AEO	M	18-55	LAL PURCH	$250
MID-VALUE	IOS	TIER 3	AEO	M	18-55	LAL PURCH	$250
MID-VALUE	AND	TIER 1	AEO	M	18-55	RPG	$250
MID-VALUE	AND	TIER 2	AEO	M	18-55	RPG	$250
MID-VALUE	AND	TIER 3	AEO	M	18-55	RPG	$250
LUCRATIVE	AND	TIER 1	AI	M	18-55	RPG	$400
LUCRATIVE	AND	TIER 2	AI	M	18-55	RPG	$400
LUCRATIVE	AND	TIER 3	AI	M	18-55	RPG	$400
LUCRATIVE	IOS	TIER 1	AEO	M	18-55	LAL PURCH	$250
LUCRATIVE	IOS	TIER 2	AEO	M	18-55	LAL PURCH	$250
LUCRATIVE	IOS	TIER 3	AEO	M	18-55	LAL PURCH	$250

A proper Facebook plan will include the following:

- **Audiences**: In the example above, each row is an audience (or "ad set") in Facebook. Each row contains pertinent details of the audience, such as the gender, age, interests, and where along the value spectrum I assume the users fall.
- **Budget allocation per audience**: Also as shown, you can see that I list how much daily budget each row (or "audience") will receive each day. *Note that your TOTAL daily Facebook budget (when adding up all ad sets, geos, OSs, etc.) should be between $500 and $3000 per day for the first week or so. This is because less than this and you won't have enough data to really learn. More than this, and you risk wasting your money on junk audiences.*
- **Geographies**: In general, go for Tier 1 countries (United States, United Kingdom, Australia, and Canada). If you are super heavily growth-oriented, then target Tier 2 as well (France, New Zealand,

Nordics, Germany, etc.). If your app has some unique, random demand in a Tier 3 country (like Mexico or Brazil) then target them too.
- **Operating System**: Your Android campaigns will be separate from your iOS campaigns. It's how Facebook is setup. If you're advertising on both OSs, then specify as such in your spreadsheet. I like to allocate OSs 50/50 so that each gets an equal chance to spend for the first few days. As data comes in, I adjust budgets up or down accordingly.

TAKE FEATURES INTO ACCOUNT WHEN PLANNING

If you expect Google Play or Apple App Store to feature your app in one of their "best of the best" type lists, and if you expect that this feature will be in a good location within the app store, rather than buried in some niche game genre or niche geography app store, then you wouldn't want to spend as much on Facebook, or any other ad network. The reason is you don't need user acquisition very much at that point. See the 'When to Use Facebook' chapter for more on this.

4

TECHNICAL SETUP

Technical setup is required to run Facebook ads. You have integrate to your tracking solution with Facebook. As a reminder, this book is a ***primer***. I will not go into extensive detail on how to do each of these, but at least you'll have a checklist, and can use your friend, the Internet, for further technical guidance.

TRACKER SETUP

Decide on a tracker

A "tracker" is like Google Analytics for mobile apps. It allows you to track monetization and retention by source. It's a must-have, as one cannot simply rely on Facebook or the app stores for this information.

Deciding on which track you choose is more of a decision for the developer and business owner to decide, but I wholeheartedly recommend AppsFlyer because it is the best in the industry. I believe it has a free version, so don't let the pricing scare you. Their service is good, their dashboards are good, and overall, they're just the industry standard for tracking mobile app performance.

Set up your tracker

Each tracking solution, such as AppsFlyer, has ample help materials to assist you in setup. Use them.

Track that installs and revenue are "tracking" correctly

After all, the tracker needs to track, right? So you have to test that the tracker SDK is functioning as expected. Each tracker has their own method for this. In AppsFlyer's case, this essentially involves downloading their testing app, opening your app build, and performing a test purchase in the app. You then log back into AppsFlyer and see if the install was logged, and that the purchase was logged. You'll know within 60 seconds, so if it's not showing up in AppsFlyer, then something is amiss. Again, check with your tracker for the very specific instructions required to complete this step.

FACEBOOK SETUP

Create the Following Basic Facebook Assets:

- Facebook Business Page
- Business Manager account
- Ads Manager account

Add Your App to Facebook

- Click here for Android instructions.
- Click here for iOS instructions.

CONNECT FACEBOOK WITH YOUR TRACKER

If you use AppsFlyer, this is super easy. Just follow these instructions. Ensure that you follow those instructions twice: once for the Android app, and once for the iOS app.

PART II. SETTING UP FACEBOOK

We're getting close to being able to run Facebook advertising! Remember that planning chapter, where you were to create a list of each desired ad set in a spreadsheet? That will come in handy here in this part of the book.

Before we get started, a few words about account structure in Facebook Ads Manager:

- *Campaigns*: Every Facebook ad account must have at least one campaign. A campaign is little more than a "folder" that holds your ad sets and ads. A campaign, however, can only have one goal. In our case, the goal is to get people to install your app. Other campaign goals include things like brand awareness, or driving traffic to a website, or converting Facebook users to buy a product from an e-commerce site, just to name a few. So, with that said, if your goal is to drive a bunch of app installs, then you could, theoretically,

get by with just one campaign. However, most people have a campaign for each OS/optimization, resulting in several campaigns per ad account. More on that in the next chapter.
- *Ad Sets*: An ad set is where you specify *who* you want to target. Each ad set can only target one OS (Android or iOS). So, if your app is on both Google Play and the Apple App Store, then you would need a minimum of two ad sets in your ad account. Yet, most advertisers have tons of ad sets. That is because sometimes the "who" you want to target could be people interested in RPG games. Other times you may want to target lookalike users. Other times you may want to target just women. There's infinite combinations of "audiences" and ad sets are where you define your audience.
- *Ads*: C'mon. We all know what an ad is. It's that pretty little video or image and catchy ad copy that you see when you're on Facebook or Instagram. Each ad set must contain at least one ad. Yet most ad sets contain between 5 and 50 ads.

5

AUDIENCE SETUP

The key advantage of Facebook, over other ad networks, is its ability to create highly targeted audiences. In Facebook Ads Manager, there are three types of audiences:

- *Saved*: When creating an ad set, sometimes we add lots and lots of interests into a single ad set. If you think you'll ever want to re-use that list, you can save the audience to save time in the future.
- *Custom*: A custom audience is one that you'll use all the time. Here, you can create an audience of users from which to build lookalikes. For instance, you can create a custom list of actual users who have opened your app in the last X number of days, or users who have made a purchase, or any number of other combinations. You can even upload an actual customer list into Facebook, though we won't go over that in this book, because it's not all that necessary thanks to Facebook's functionality.
- *Lookalike*: From a custom audience, we can build what's called a "Lookalike" audience, which is an

audience that looks like your custom audience. These are gold. These are what put Facebook's Ad Manager on the map. For example, if you created a custom audience of actual users who made a purchase, say in the last 30 days, you can create a lookalike audience to find more people who have the same traits of those purchasers.

NAVIGATING TO YOUR AUDIENCE LIBRARY

When logged into your Facebook Business Manager (which is business.facebook.com) then, regardless of what screen you are on, you can head over to your audiences library by clicking "Audiences" as shown below:

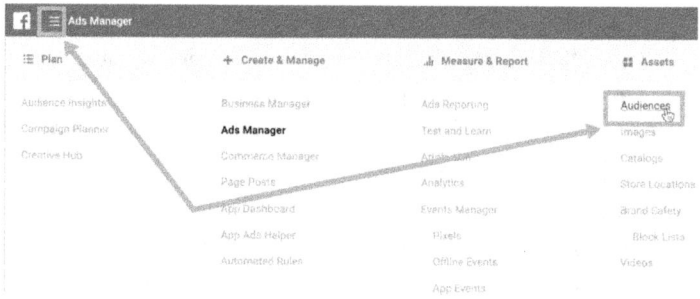

Then, you should arrive on a page that looks something like this:

HOW TO RUN FACEBOOK ADVERTISING FOR YOUR ... | 17

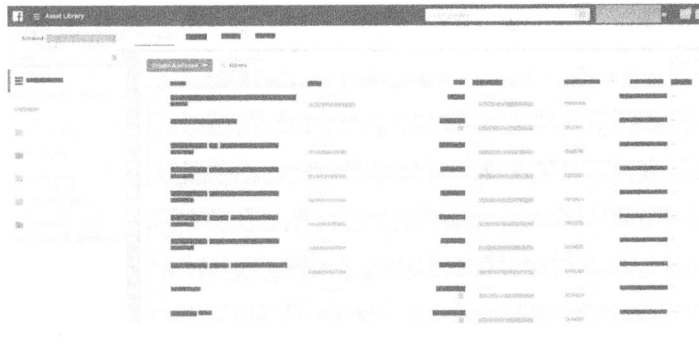

SAVED AUDIENCES

As mentioned earlier, when you are setting up your ad set (see next chapter), and you select the countries, ages, genders, and interests you would like, you have the option, right there in the ad set window pane, to save the audience. When you do save it, you will see it in your Audience Library. You will also be able to retrieve the saved audience at the ad set level, when creating a new ad set, as shown below:

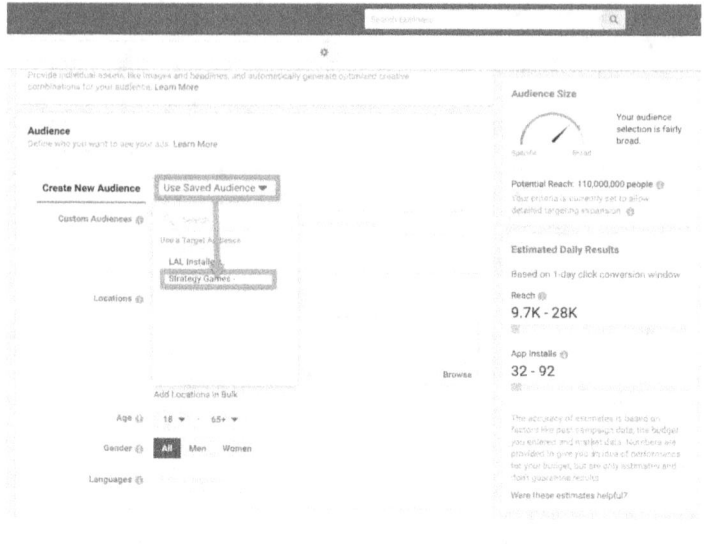

CUSTOM AUDIENCES

A custom audience is 99% of the time utilized as a "seed" audience from which to create a Lookalike Audience. One can get pretty clever with defining a custom audience. Navigate to your Audience Library and click "Create Audience" and from there, select "Custom Audience" from the dropdown as shown below:

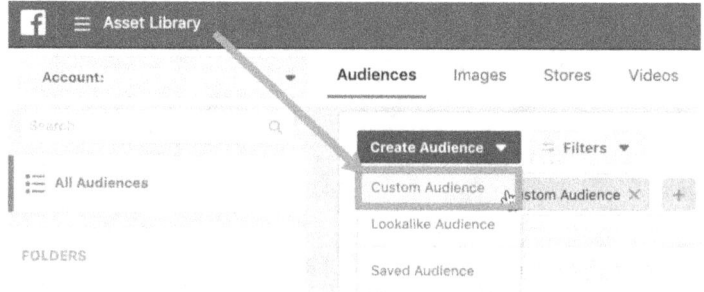

Next, select "App Activity" as shown below:

Select your desired parameters and click save, as shown below:

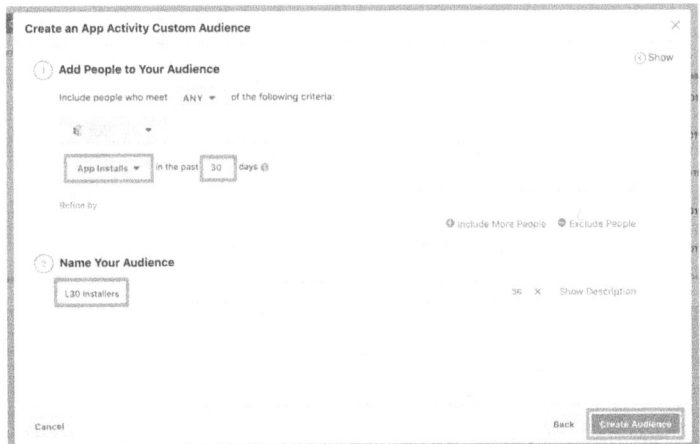

Note: It sometimes takes custom audiences up to 24 hours to propagate. I recommend creating this audience(s) and then creating your Lookalike Audience the following day.

I commonly create the following three custom audiences to serve as "seed audiences" for Lookalikes:

Last 30-Day Installers Custom Audience:

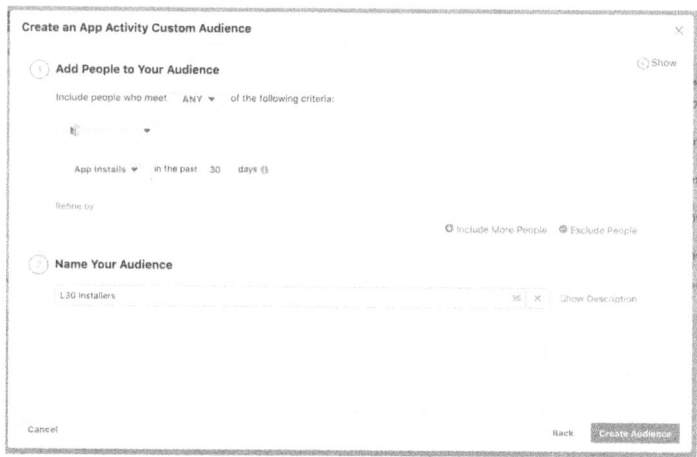

Last 30-Day Purchasers Custom Audience:

HOW TO RUN FACEBOOK ADVERTISING FOR YOUR ... | 21

10% Most Active Users Custom Audience:

LOOKALIKE AUDIENCES OR LAL

Once you have created a custom audience to serve as a "seed audience", you are ready to create a Lookalike Audience. Navigate to your Audience Library and click "Create Audience" and from there, select "Lookalike Audience" from the dropdown as shown below:

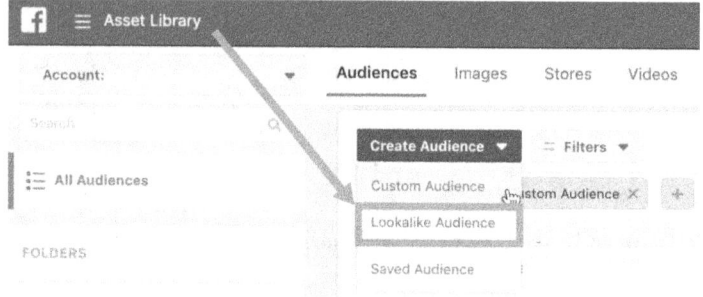

Specify your parameters as shown below:

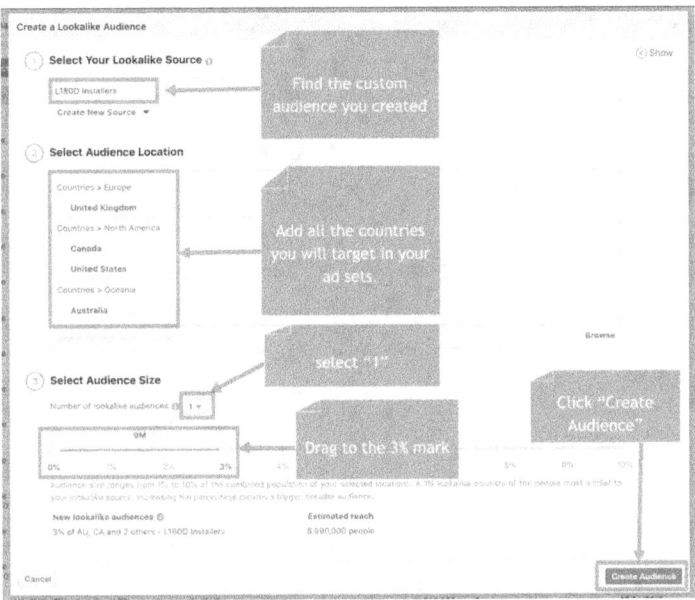

Allow the lookalike audience several hours to propagate before creating an ad set based on the lookalike. Once the it's been several hours, you can select it at the ad set level in Ads Manager as shown below:

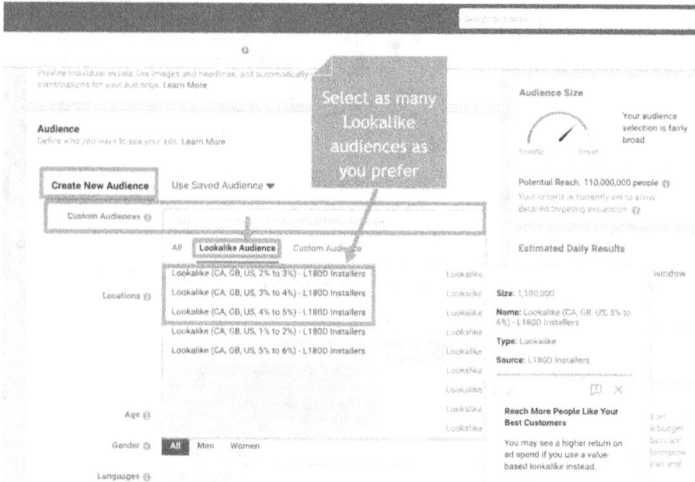

Note: don't forget to add your desired countries. Just because you selected certain countries when building your lookalike audience, doesn't mean your ads will serve in those countries. The only way to serve your ads in those countries is to select those countries at the ad set level.

CAMPAIGN SETUP

CREATE A CAMPAIGN

Navigate to your Facebook Business Manager at business.facebook.com and from there navigate to Ads Manager as shown below:

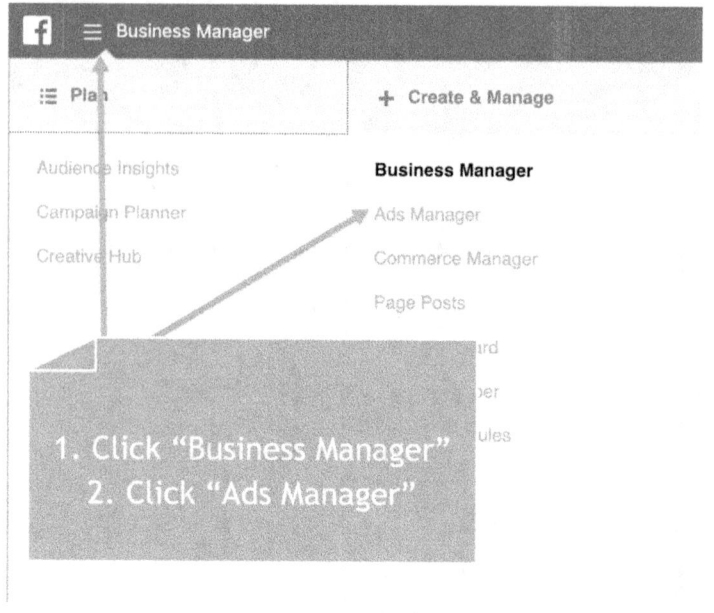

Click 'Campaigns' as shown below:

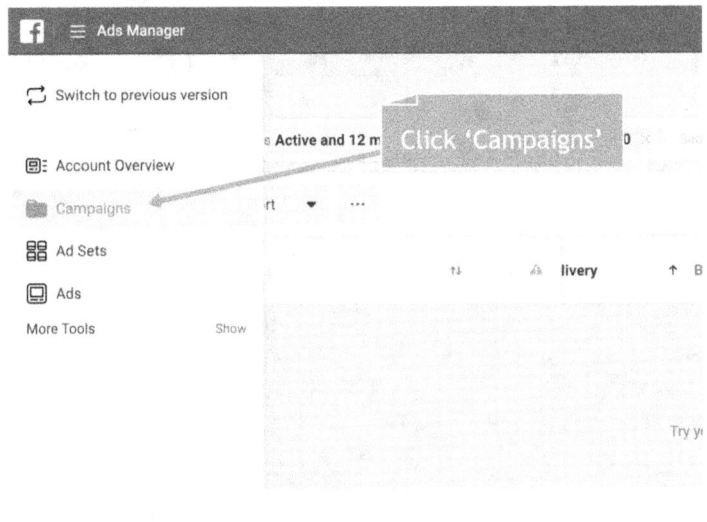

Click 'Create' as shown below:

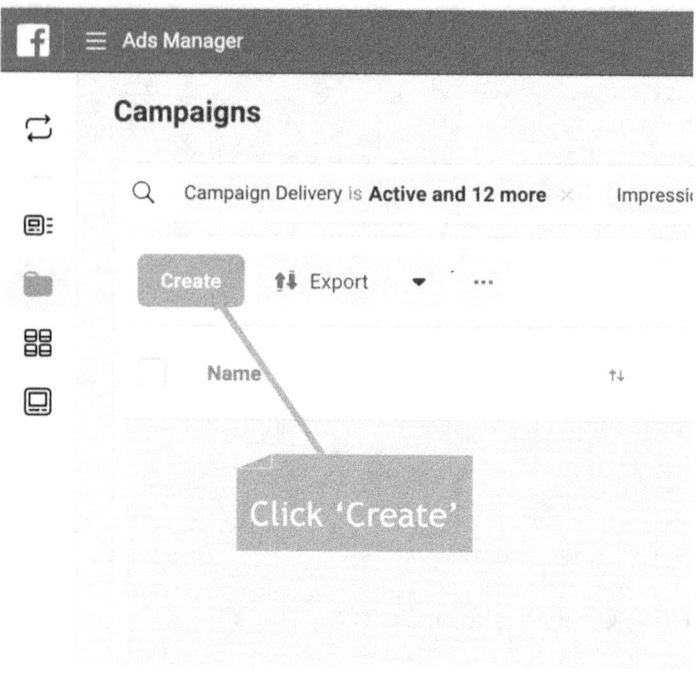

Select 'App installs' as the objective:

[Screenshot of Facebook campaign creation interface with overlay text: "Choose 'App installs' as your campaign marketing objective"]

Give your campaign a name, following a commonly-used naming pattern of {Goal}_{OS}.

For example, your campaign name might be "AEO_AND" for Android campaigns or "AEO_iOS" for iOS campaigns. As a reminder, Facebook does not allow you to serve ads for both Android and iOS in the same campaigns, so that's why in my example above, I have an Android campaign and an iOS campaign.

The three {Goal} options are shown below. You'll have no idea what I'm talking about right now. I'll explain in the next section of this chapter, at which point, this will all make sense. See the three options below:

- AEO if the goal is App Event Optimization
- AI if the goal is App Install. Note that the campaign marketing objective is always "App Install", but there

is a secondary ad set setting, which we'll review momentarily, which is also App Install. Don't be confused. Hang in there.
- VO if the goal is Value Optimized

Click 'Continue':

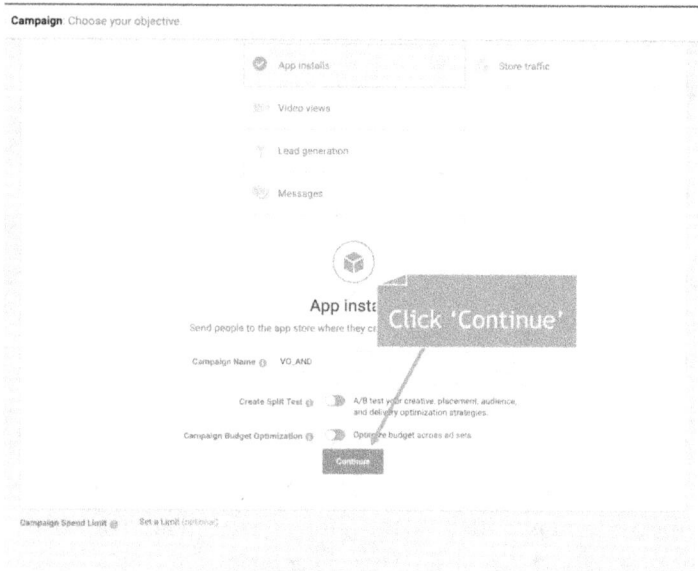

That's it. Your first campaign has been created. But you must populate the campaign with an ad set (which describes the audience and demographics) as well as ads (which is what will actually be shown to someone. See sections below.

7

AD SET SETUP

Give your ad set a name following this commonly-used naming convention: {Goal}_{OS}_{Interest}_{Gender}_{Age}_{Geo}. Your ad set name might look something along the lines of what we see in the image below:

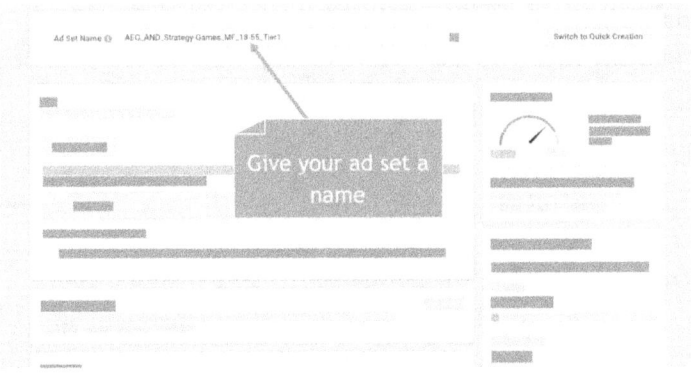

Pro tips based on the image above:

- **Gender:** Set gender to "MF" so you target both

genders. If Facebook sees one gender outperforms another, it's very smart at reallocating spend towards the best gender.
- **Age**: Set age to 18-65. Facebook will go after the best age group. So don't stress too much about what age you should target.
- **Geographies**: If your goal is to acquire users who actually make a purchase - and 99% of the time that's the goal - then select quality geos. Most of the time, this means only targeting United States, United Kingdom, Canada, and Australia. These four geos are loosely referred to as "Tier 1".

Select your desired app store and app as shown below. Select "Google Play" if this campaign/ad set is for Android. Select "iTunes" if this campaign/ad set is for iOS. Never select "iTunes for iPad", even if you intend to target iPad users. It's a misleading choice, and don't bother considering it. See image below for reference:

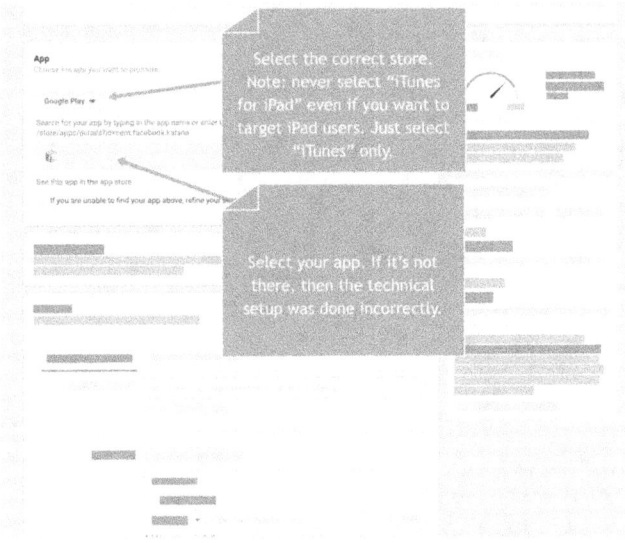

Select your desired countries. Don't get fancy by only selecting major cities or states. Doing so will cause your cost per app install to skyrocket. I recommend targeting US/UK/CA/AU for reasons mentioned above. See image below:

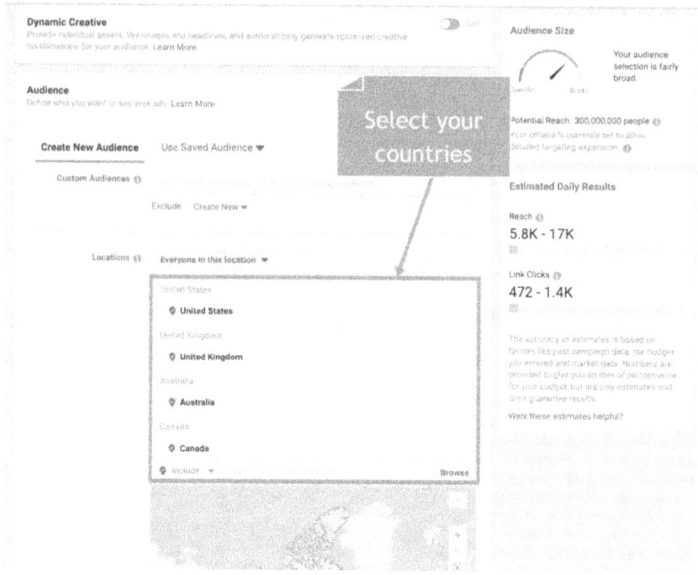

Select your desired age range and gender. I recommend leaving it at the default. Also, don't specify a language. It will increase your cost per app install, and it's unnecessary anyway. The only time you'd specify a language is if you're targeting a minority language. For example, if your app is in Spanish only, and we want to acquire Spanish users in the United States, we'd select Spanish as a language. No one does this, so leave it alone:

Next, exclude anyone who has used your app. Facebook advertising for mobile apps is all about acquiring users, known as "user acquisition". We don't re-advertise to people who have already installed the app. You exclude these folks by selecting "Add a connection type". You then scroll to the very bottom of that little dialogue box, and select "Advanced combinations". From there you select your app in the little box titled "Exclude people who are connected to". Start typing your app name and it will appear. Don't worry about excluding people connected to your page - just your app. Just because someone's connected to your page, doesn't mean they have ever used your app. In fact if they are connected to your page, and have not used your app, then they're a "hot lead" and we most certainly want to target them. See image below:

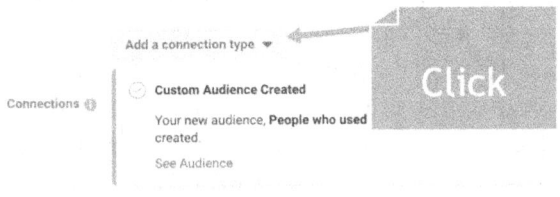

Now, scroll back up just a little, so that you can populate the "Detailed Targeting" section as shown in the next image below. This is going to be your "interest" section. It's important because it helps Facebook narrow down who it should go after.

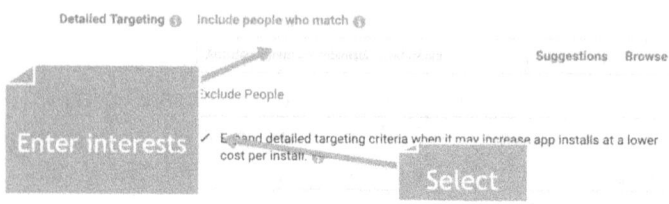

This section can feel overwhelming at first, so I'm sharing a few of the types of interests I go after:

- *Mobile Games interest*: sometimes it's worth selecting the catch-all 'Mobile game' interest. This may not monetize very well, but is an easy start.
- *Competitor interests*: If your app is similar to Angry Birds - for example - you would want to target people who have an interest in 'Angry Birds' or anything similar. Do a little research to find out your competitors, and then see if they appear as an interest in Facebook. Add as many interests as you can, but don't use the "narrow" functionality this will cause your cost per install to be too high. *Note: You can find out your competitors in many ways. One easy way is to go to the app stores, pull up a known competitor, and look at all the recommended apps. Another way is to use a tool like AppAnnie to see similar games based on genre. More on that later.*
- *Genre interest*: Rather than listing every possible competitor, sometimes it's just as effective to select your genre. So, if you have a simulation game, select that as an interest. If you have a city-builder game,

select that. If you have an epic RPG, select that. You get the point. Facebook will go after anyone who likes those genres.
- *Casual games interest (or mid-core, or hard-core)*: Most apps are for casual players, rather than folks who play at hours at a stretch. If your game falls into this category (which is technically its own genre), then select 20 or 30 casual games even if they have nothing to do with your app. There's usually shared interest among these types of users. The concept is the same if your game is for mid- or hard-core users.
- *Facebook suggestions interest*: See the little "Suggestions" text in the next image below? This is a super handy way to find interests you may not have considered before. Type a few interests you know are on-target and then click the little "Suggestions" button for more ideas.

Ensure that you select that little checkbox that says "Expand detailed targeting criteria….". This will help ensure your audience is large and your cost per install is low. Facebook still does a good job at acquiring users that are related to your desired interests, even though you're relaxing your controls.

Check that your audience size is large enough. At a very minimum, you need about 50,000, but ideally over 1 million. If your audience is over 20 million then you should probably narrow down your targeting if you can so Facebook has more direction:

38 | MICHAEL B. CASTILLE

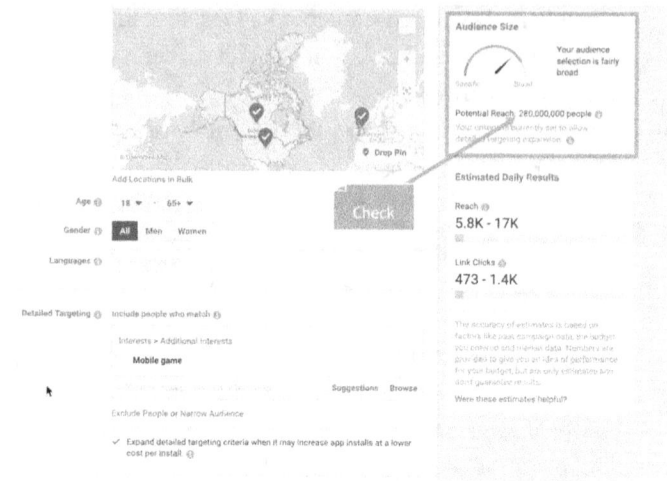

In the "Placements" section, there are three areas to keep in mind:

- **Automatic Placements**: Keep this selected. This will increase your reach.
- **Minimum OS Version**: Go to the the app store page for your app. Scroll down until you get the details area that tells you who the developer is, when the app was last released, and the minimum OS version. and check the minimum OS version requirements. If it's an Android campaign, then go to the Google Play store. If it's an iOS campaign, go to the Apple App Store.
- **Wifi checkbox**: While you're at the app store page for your app, see how big the app file size is. If it's over 200 MB, then it's probably safe to check that little box. After all, most people don't want to use up their mobile data to download your app. If you serve them

HOW TO RUN FACEBOOK ADVERTISING FOR YOUR ... | 39

an ad while they're connected to wifi, then it's no problem for them.

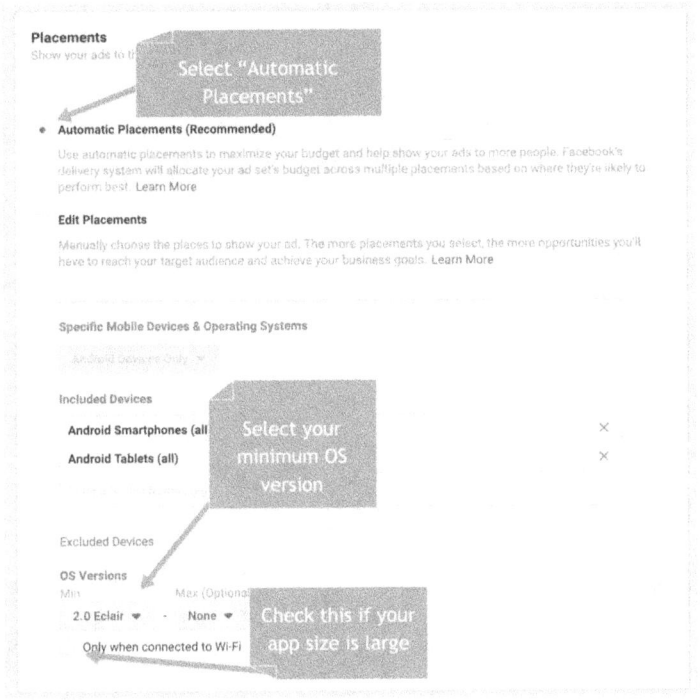

Next, you will complete the "Budget and Schedule" section. Ensure all your settings are as shown in the image below, with the only "variable" being the budget.

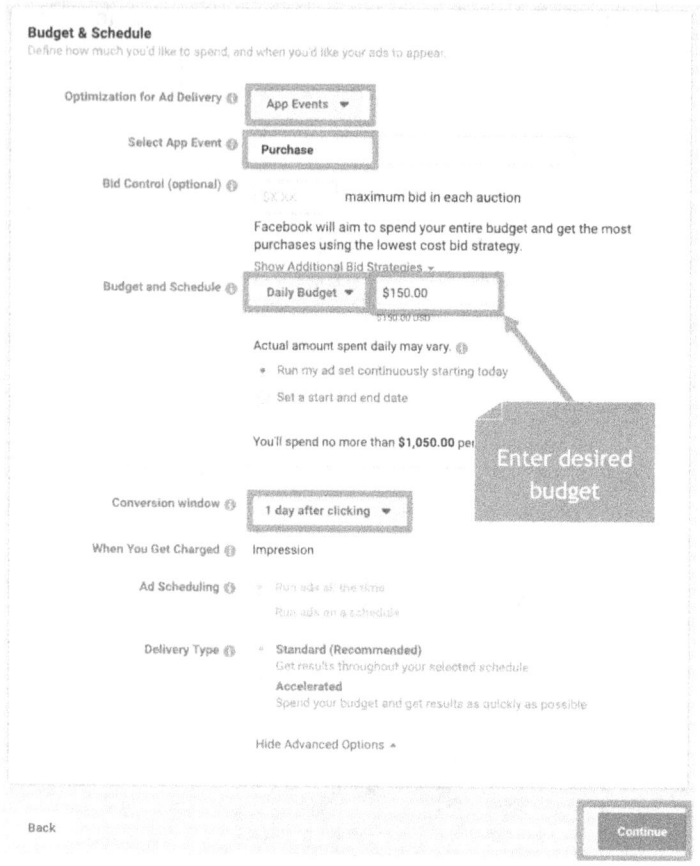

A few words about each of the components of the image above:

Optimization for Ad Delivery section:

- ***App Events***: This is known as "AEO" which stands for

"App Event Optimization". This optimization is the best because Facebook targets app installers likely to make a purchase. And after all, isn't that the whole point?

- ***App Installs***: In very rare cases, you won't care about optimizing for AEO. Rather, you'll want to target the cheapest app installers, without concerning yourself whether or not they'll make a purchase. This is known as "AI". Soft launches are a great time to optimize towards AI, when you're working to get your retention to a healthy state. Otherwise, there's not much point.
- ***Link Clicks***: Useless. Ignore.
- ***Value Optimized***: You won't see this option right away, because Facebook needs to accumulate lots of user data from your ads to know who is purchasing what. This is known as a "VO" campaign. This one notch fancier than the AEO optimization because rather than go after "any ole purchaser" Facebook goes after "whales" which are users likely to make a ton of purchasers. Basically they go after people most likely to become fanatical about your game. In general, the cost of installs are much higher for VO than AEO, but the returns on ad spend are usually much higher too. This optimization doesn't work for all advertisers so use with caution.

Select App Event:

When you select the "App Events" optimization just discussed, you'll need to tell Facebook what kind of event you want. This is a book about how to market your mobile game. Therefore, games need to have purchases. Select the purchase event. If you don't see it, then your technical setup was incorrect. See the section about integrating Facebook and AppsFlyer.

Budget and Schedule:

Select "Daily Budget" rather than "Lifetime Budget". In the world of mobile games, you want to optimize on a daily basis.

Next, you'll input your desired budget. If it's an AI campaign, it can have a minimum daily budget of $25. If it's AEO, a minimum daily budget of $100 (though Facebook recommends much higher). If it's VO, a minimum daily budget of $250.

Conversion Window:

Start with '1 day after clicking', but in the 'Best Practices' chapter, I'll show you how to determine if your conversion window should actually be 7 days.

You have now created an ad set. Rinse and repeat these steps for all desired ad sets. As a reminder, a best practice is to keep all Android ad sets in an Android campaign, and all iOS ad sets in an iOS campaign.

8

AD SETUP

Give your ad a name. I recommend using the following naming convention: {concept}_{format}_{orientation}. So for example, in the image below, the "concept is character level up" and the format is "video" rather than "image", and the orientation is "square" rather than "portrait" or "landscape".

Select your Facebook page and Instagram page. While you must have a Facebook page, an instagram page is optional:

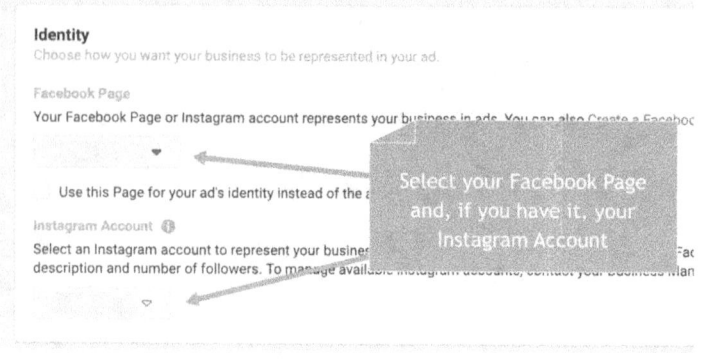

Select your ad format. I normally just upload a single image or video, rather than carousels or Instant Experience, but it's worth testing to see how the various formats respond.

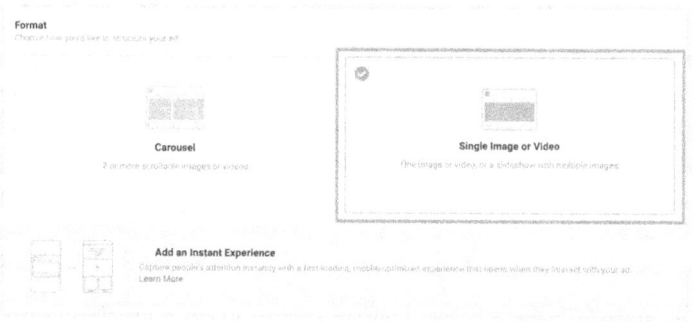

Specify whether you're uploading an image or video. Next, upload your content. Ignore all the other confusing settings and recommendations you see on this image, as they're not that important.

HOW TO RUN FACEBOOK ADVERTISING FOR YOUR ... | 45

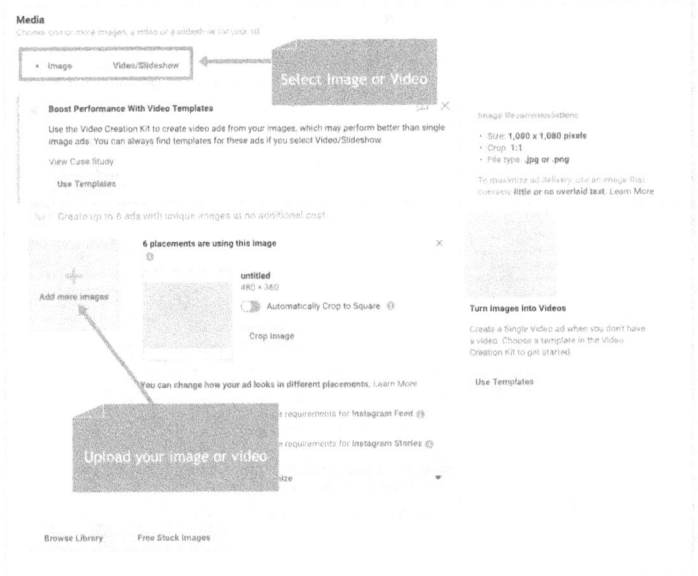

Note: Facebook's complete ad size specifications can be found here: https://www.facebook.com/business/ads-guide I never use this, because it's *way* too overwhelming. I have acquired millions of app installs for many kinds of apps, across every placement (Facebook, Instagram, Audience Network) and have never had any issues using the following super simple information:

Image Landscape Dimensions: 1200x628 pixels

Image Square Dimensions: 600x600 pixels

Video Landscape Dimensions: 1920x1080 pixels

Video Square Dimensions: 600x600 pixels

Video Portrait Dimensions: 1080x1920 pixels

. . .

Pro Tip: If your game is mainly played holding the phone sideways, then focus on creating square and landscape ads. If your phone is mainly played holding the phone in the normal position, then focus mainly on creating square and portrait ads. Yet, if you can, create all three orientations, so that you can test to see which ones drive the best results.

Create brief ad copy and headline and a call to action. Use emojis to get attention. Visit emojicopy.com to search relevant emojis. Grab ad copy from your app store page if you need approved copy or inspiration. I recommend using only the call to action "Play Game" since that's what the app is - a game.

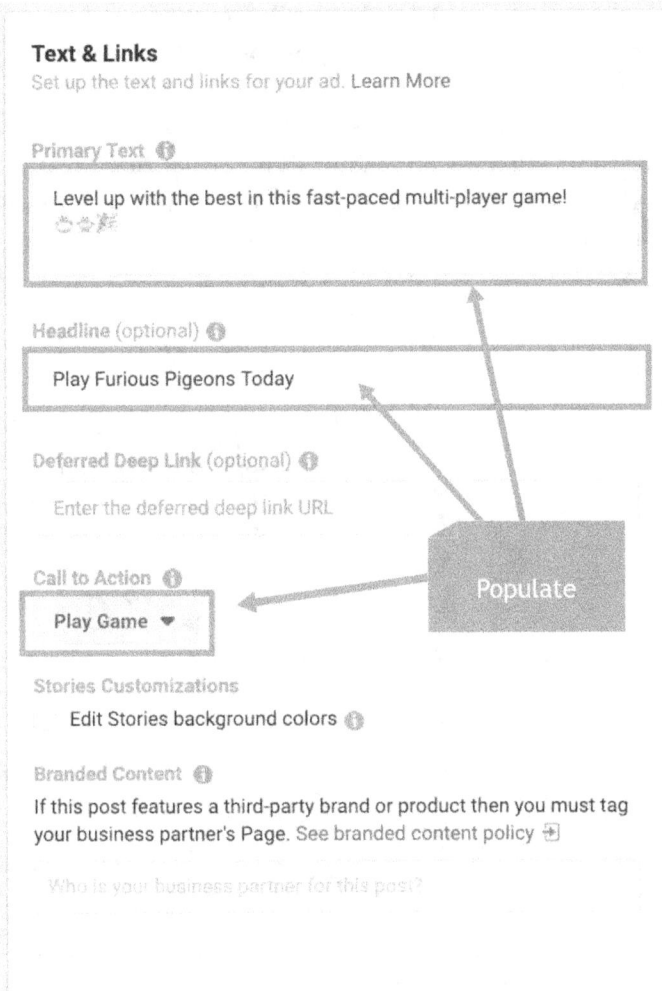

Check that your ad looks fine on all placements as shown below. Your ad size/format may not be available for all placements, and when this is the case, Facebook will let you know as you scroll through each placement preview. This is fine. Facebook just won't show this particular ad for that particular placement. There's no further action required on your part.

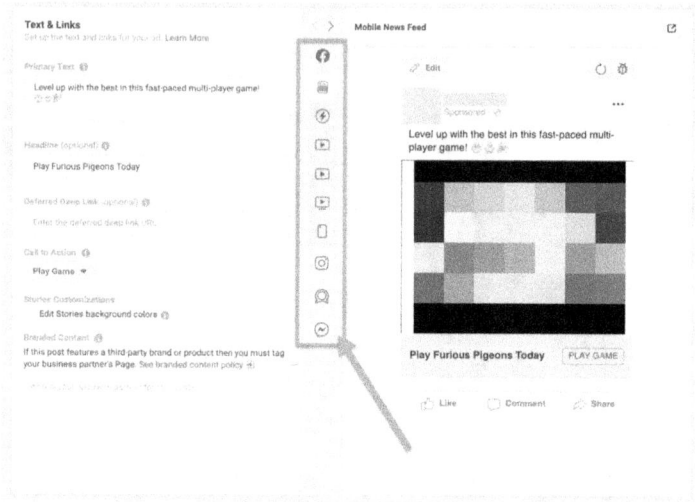

If you would like to serve the ad in another language, first check that your app is localized to that language. It does no good to show Spanish ad copy if, upon downloading the app, the user finds that everything is in English. Yet, if the ad is in fact localized for another language, and you would like to serve ads to that language, then select the "Create in Different Languages" button and follow the prompts. This is known as Dynamic Language Optimization (DLO), and Facebook detects the language the user has set on their laptop. If it matches the language you have uploaded, then they will see an ad.

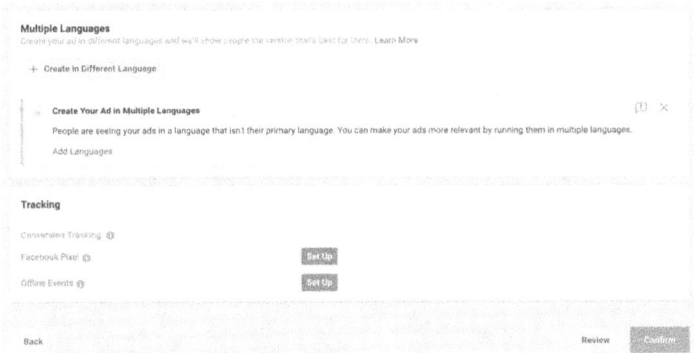

That's it! Your ad has now been created! Make sure this ad has been added to all active ad sets. Use the "duplicate" feature to make this is a little easier.

PART III. CAMPAIGN MANAGEMENT

The goal of campaign management is to make sure your advertising budget is promoting the best audiences and creatives. This part of the book will show you how to do a good job at this. With that said, I should point out that the entire scope of Facebook campaign management for mobile app games far exceeds what we cover in this book, which, as a reminder, is a *primer*.

9

COLUMN SETUP

Before we can manage our account, we must specify the correct columns. Navigate to the columns area as shown and click "Customize Columns":

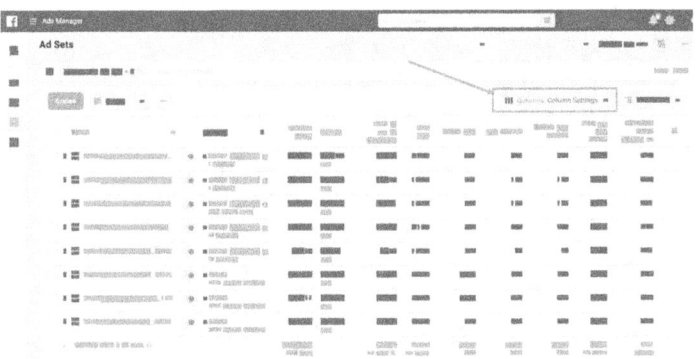

Next, select the following columns, being sure to give this preset column group a name before saving, as shown:

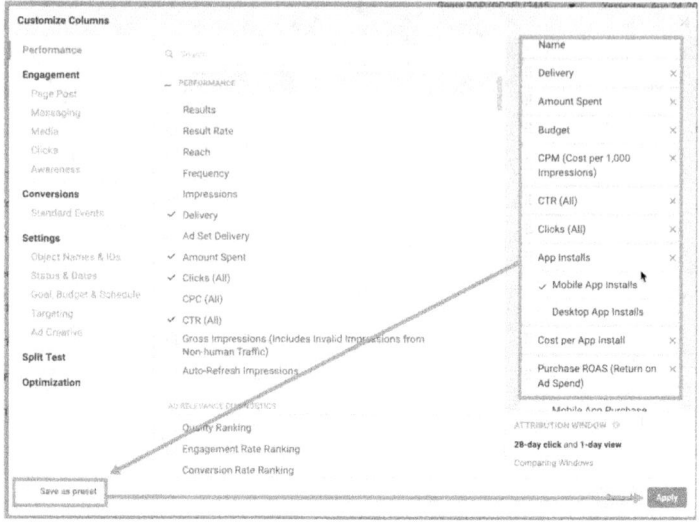

Now we are ready to begin managing the campaigns!

10

DAILY MANAGEMENT

Every day, you'll need to do the following to ensure your ad sets are in good working order. Navigate to the ad set level view, **adjust your date to "yesterday"** and pull up your saved column set that we discussed in the previous chapter. Then do the following:

DELIVERY AUDIT

Audit the delivery of all of the ad sets. This should take all of about five seconds, but doing so will let you know if there's any issue, such as ads not delivering due to being rejected. You want the delivery to say "Active" or "Active (Learning)".

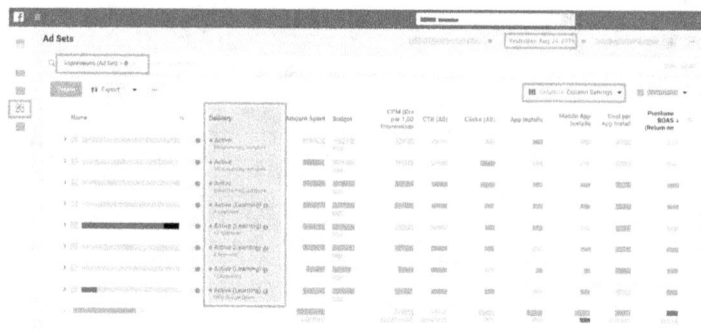

RETURN ON AD SPEND OR ROAS

Next, sort all ad sets in descending order by the Purchase ROAS column. Because we're looking at "yesterday" data, we can think of this as Day 1 data. By contrast, if we were looking at data from three days ago, we would consider that as Day 3 data. Looking at Day 1 data, or data from yesterday, we classify ad sets as either "above average" or "below average" depending on whether they fall above or below to the cumulative average shown in bold on the bottom row:

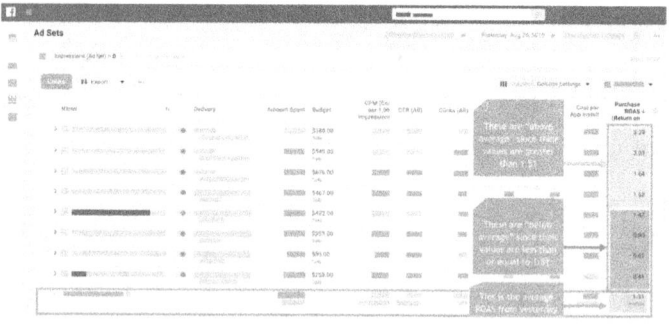

For the "above average" ad sets, adjust those daily budgets by

30%. For those not as mathematically inclined, multiply the budget by 1.3. So, for example, if an ad set's current budget is $380, then $380 x 1.3 = $494.

For the "below average" ad sets, reduce the spend to 70% of the current budget. You do this by multiplying the budget by 0.7. So for example, if an ad set's current budget is $380, then $380 x 0.7 = $266.

Day by day, you'll start to spend more and more towards the good ad sets, and less and less towards the bad ones.

SPOT-CHECKING OTHER KPIS

Each day, in addition to adjusting budgets based on ROAS, make sure you peek at the Cost per App Install to ensure that no ad set has an exorbitant CPI. If it does, check if any ad is driving up the cost. If you can't find a justifying reason, then pause the ad set.

BENCHMARKS

So, what are good KPIs to aim for? This depends on the following main factors:

- **Game genre**: Hard core games monetize slower than casual games because it takes a while for the user to really get engaged. Do some web research to find metrics that are more in line with your genre.
- **Geographies targeted**: The information shown below is for Tier 1 geographies (United States, United Kingdom, Canada, Australia)
- **Age of the game**: Any game that's been in the tier 1 geos for over two years is an "old" game. Results may not be as strong for older games.

With that said, these are general ballpark figures to at least know you're on the right track, and are helpful for any genre, of any game age, for Tier 1 geographies.

- **Retention**: Day 1 retention: 25-35%
- **CPM** (or cost per thousand impressions): $5-15.

Anything higher than this and you have a super competitive audience or else horrible Facebook performance. Either of those two factors can hurt your CPM.
- **CTR** (or click-through rate): 0.4%-2.0%. Anything less than this warrants either (a) better targeting, (b) better ad creative, or (c) test dynamic creative optimization, which is discussed in the 'Cool Features chapter.
- **CVR** (or conversion rate), where a "conversion" in this benchmark is the installs divided by clicks as shown in Facebook: 25-65%. Yep, that's a huge variation, but it's true. Anything less than 25% and you're either (a) targeting the wrong users, (b) major disconnected between your ad copy/creative and the app store, (c) your app store needs work.
- **CPI** (or cost per install): $0.50 to $10. Again, that's a huge variation. AI ad sets will be $0.50 to $3.00. AEO will be $1.50 to $6.00. VO ad sets will be $2 to $10. Note: if you don't understand AI/AEO/VO, then see Part 2: Setting Up Facebook for more information.
- **Yesterday ROAS**: This metric is absolutely the most volatile metric, in the sense that it varies wildly with the factors mentioned at the beginning of this chapter. Yet, there are some general pieces of information that I can tell you from experience, raise a red flag of concern. If your "yesterday" ROAS in Facebook is less than 0.03 (which means 3%) then that's a red flag that something is wrong with your game. Most genres/games/etc/ lie somewhere between 0.10 and 0.50 (or 10 and 50%) when looking at yesterday. Some even do much better. If your ROAS for any ad set is consistently 0.03 when checking your ad sets every day for several days, then

(a) you need to check that your ad set optimization is AEO rather than something like AI, (b) check that your CPI isn't crazy high, because if that's high, then it could be eating into your profits [if it's crazy high, see if it's the CPM, CTR, or CVR that is out of line and work to remedy the broken metric], (c) check that your are targeting good audiences, (d) check that there's nothing wrong with the game itself.

12

WEEKLY MANAGEMENT

Each Monday, conduct a weekly analysis. Doing this on Mondays allows you to make adjustments early in the week so your week finishes strong.

BENCHMARK ANALYSIS

Have you read the "Benchmarks" chapter? If not, go back and read that real quick, because you'll need those benchmarks at your fingertips for your weekly campaign management activities. Each Monday, adjust your Facebook date range to the full week before (Monday through Sunday), and check the following information for each ad set:

- ***Benchmark Analysis for Ad Sets***: For each ad set, check if the CPM, CTR, CVR, and CPIs are healthy. Don't worry so much about ROAS right now. If anything looks way out of the ordinary, then check my recommendations as to how you can repair the "broken" KPI.

- **Benchmark Analysis for Ads**: Now for every single ad, look at only those that have spent more than 1% of your overall Facebook account-level spend from last week. If last week, you spent $29,284 in Facebook, then you want to take a look at any that spent at least $292 ($29,284 * 0.01 = $292). If any of these ads had way out of whack KPIs consider pausing them if and only if their ROAS is below the weekly average.

TEST NEW AUDIENCES

Each Monday, I recommend launching two new iOS audiences and two new Android audiences. If it's an AI campaign, put each budget at $50/day. If AEO, then $100, if VO, then $150. Let these "newbies" run for Monday and Tuesday, and only on Wednesday will you make any adjustments to budgets.

APP STORE ANALYSIS

Go to your app store pages on Google Play and iTunes and read about 10 or 15 of the most recent reviews. Doing so will, over time, keep you in the loop of what your customers are saying. I have also received many targeting ideas simply from reading comments. A user may, for example, comment that your game reminds them of another game. Great. That's a new interest you can target on Facebook. Repeat this exercise for a couple of your competitors.

APPANNIE ANALYSIS

AppAnnie is an awesome free tool that will provide much information about not just your app, but your competitors.

Sign up for a free account, and then, when logged in, search for your app as shown below:

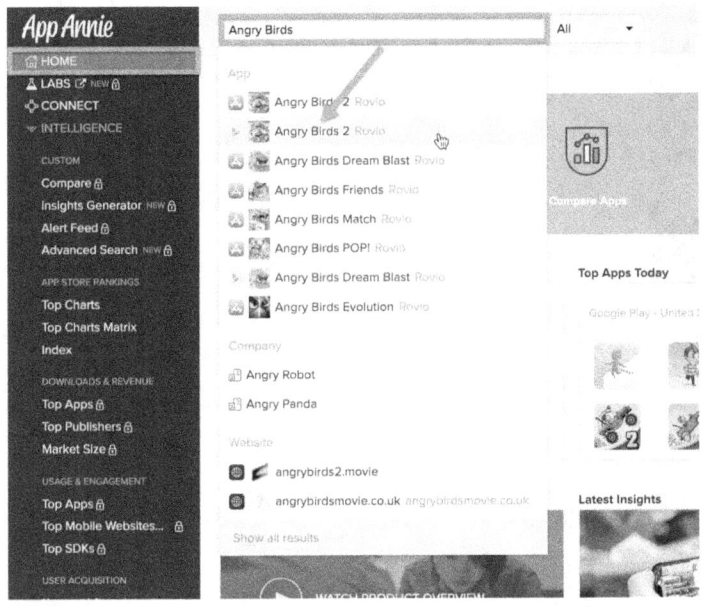

Check if your app was featured, and do the same for your competitors:

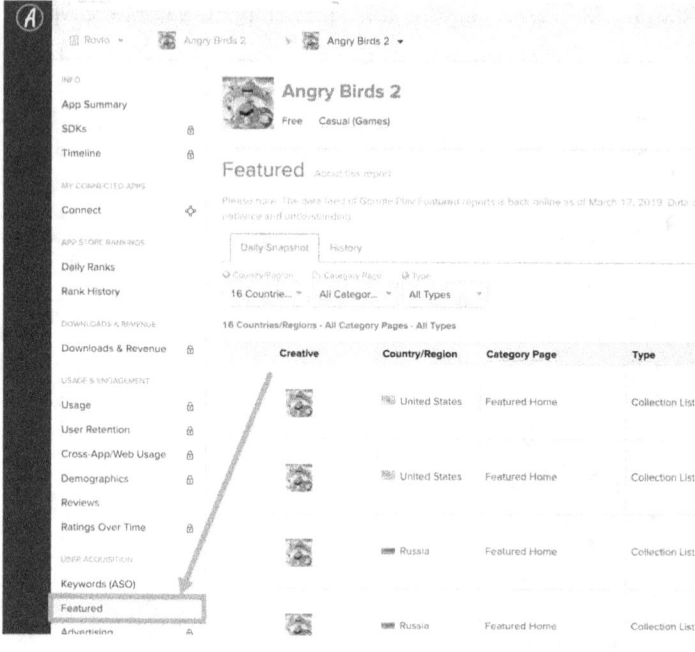

Also check out the "App Summary" page to check if there were any app updates and what the nature of the update was. This is great for checking on your competitors too.

PART IV. TIPS AND TRICKS

13

BEST PRACTICES

BUDGETS

It's important to set a sufficiently high budget so that Facebook accumulates enough learnings to know who to go after. They always recommend much higher budgets than necessary - for the most part. For AI ad sets, use at least $25/day. but sweet spot is about $100. AEO needs at least $100/day but sweet spot is $250. VO needs at least $250/day but sweet spot is $5000.

AUDIENCE SIZE

Just as Facebook needs a sufficiently large budget for its learnings, so too, it needs a sufficiently large audience size from which to learn. For AI, the ideal is 200k. For AEO, the ideal is 2 million. For VO the ideal is 10 million.

RESULTS

Each ad set needs to receive at least 50 results per week in order for Facebook's algorithm to optimize. A "result" is defined by your optimization. For AI, the result is an install. For AEO or VO, the result is a purchase. Select the "Results" column and check this periodically.

AUDIENCE OVERLAP

When two or more ad sets target the same group of people, or if one ad set targets *some* of the same people in another ad set, then you have "audience overlap". It happens all the time. Yet sometimes, it can become a problem. If an ad set has more than ~20% audience overlap with another ad set, then this can cause higher costs per install which can eat into your profits. Check "Delivery Insights" for each ad set to ensure that you don't have audience overlap. More on Delivery Insights in the "Cool Features" chapter.

RETARGETING

In the web world, retargeting is a core strategy. We retarget everyone. Didn't make a purchase? There's a campaign for that. Just made a purchase? There's an up-sell campaign for that. Haven't purchased in a while? There's a re-engagement campaign for that.

Yet with mobile app marketing for games, retargeting isn't that big of a deal. When you do retarget in Facebook, your campaign "goal" is conversions rather than app installs. And your list is not a set of interests, but rather you create a custom audience of all purchasers, making sure to have an exclusion list, alongside the purchase list, that excludes anyone who purchased in the last 14 days.

Typically, retargeting is an adequate strategy when there is a new event within the game, such as a holiday event, or more levels added.

However, it's hard to spend your retargeting budget on Facebook these days. There are better networks for that. Yet, if you really want to retarget your users, wait for at least 60 days after you first start advertising, and then test how retargeting performs for you. In AppsFlyer, you navigate to the re-engagement section to check your revenue, rather than the main dashboard (which is reserved for new user acquisition). Do a web search for more information on this, as this is not nearly as an exciting a topic as it may sound (from a revenue standpoint) and it's outside the scope of the book.

MERGE MULTIPLE "AUDIENCES" INTO A SINGLE AD SET

Rather than having a separate audience for every little setting (a strategy that works pretty well in web marketing), one should err on the side of merging rather than excluding. For example, merge your Tier 1 geos into a single ad set, rather than having a US ad set, a UK ad set, a Canada ad set or an Australian ad set. This gives Facebook more flexibility and they can respond in real-time to changing market conditions. If Australia is suddenly "hot" they'll allocate more spend. If it bombs for a few days, Facebook will pull back it's spend.

Other areas to merge include ages, genders, platforms, and even interests.

DON'T EXCLUDE DEMOGRAPHICS

This is similar to the previous best practice. If you think your game skews more towards young males, you can still go ahead and target females as well as older folks. This is because Facebook is very adept at not wasting your budget on the wrong folks. Why take the risk of missing out on certain demographics, when Facebook does all the analysis for you?

ADJUST BUDGETS A LITTLE PER DAY

If you want to increase your budgets, increase each ad set no more than about 30% per day. More than this, and the algorithm will be totally confused for several days, and in fact, may not ever recover the same great performance.

USE LOOKALIKE AUDIENCES WHERE POSSIBLE

In general, lookalike audiences perform better than interest-based audiences, both in terms of CPI and ROAS. But not always. See the 'Audience Setup' chapter for more information.

A LOOKALIKE SEED AUDIENCE SHOULD IDEALLY BE BETWEEN 3,000 AND 50,000 PEOPLE

When you build custom audiences, from which to "seed" a lookalike audience, make sure your seed audience (which is the "custom audience") is at least 3,000 people. Sure, you can get by with much less than this, but Facebook's algorithm will have a hard time optimizing. Also, if your seed audience is higher than 50,000 then it's too broad for Facebook, most likely. If your seed audience rests outside these parameters then check your ad set performance closely, and if it's not to your liking, then refine your custom audience.

DON'T INCREASE ANY AD SET'S BUDGET BY MORE THAN 30% PER DAY

Doing so can seriously confuse Facebook's algorithm and sometimes the issue is irreparable. Just go in each day, and increase by 10-30% each daily budget. In a matter of days, this will become exponentially higher. You just have to be patient. Even scaling down too much can confuse Facebook, so I either pause an ad set altogether if I hate the performance, or if performance is just okay but not great, then I keep only 50-70% of the daily budget.

A/B SPLIT TESTING

Facebook has a cool little A/B testing feature. Let's say you want to test two totally different ad concepts and force each ad to receive an equal amount of spend. You can't put these ads in the same ad set because Facebook skews spend towards the best ad (which I prefer, anyway). So you would put one concept in ad set "A" and create a duplicate ad set "B" with the other concept. You'd want to split the budgets 50/50 and let it run until Facebook notifies you that you have a winner.

I normally split test major ad concepts like this when I really must know which one is the statistically significant winner. Otherwise, I put the new concepts in the existing ad sets.

I also normally run a split test to compare which conversion window is best for AEO campaigns. Is it the 1-day conversion window or the 7-day? A split test can answer this.

When I have a super large app, like over 500MB, I like to a/b test one ad set with the wifi box checked, and one without. See 'Ad Set Setup' for more information.

Otherwise, I don't go crazy with A/B testing, since I like to rapidly optimize budgets daily, and you can't do that so easily with ad sets right in the middle of an a/b test.

Click here to learn more.

14

COOL FEATURES

Here's a few cool features that may be of interest to you. They're not (at the time of this writing) mandatory, so consider these optional or advanced features:

CAMPAIGN BUDGET OPTIMIZATION OR CBO

This feature allows Facebook to automatically optimize your ad sets based on performance, rather than you manually checking them each day. So far, I have found that this feature doesn't hurt performance, but only occasionally does it seem to outperform me. More info here: https://www.facebook.com/business/help/153514848493595

DYNAMIC CREATIVE OPTIMIZATION OR DCO

This is a cool feature that can improve your CTR, CVR and CPI. The idea is that rather than allowing an ad set to have multiple ads, you have a single ad, with this ad having several heading variants, primary text variants, call to action variants, and creative variants. Facebook rotates each combination resulting in better performance. The downsides are:

- Reporting is more complex, making it much more tedious to understand what's working.
- A DCO ad can only have a limited number of creatives per ad, and often your company will have many more creatives you'd like to simultaneously run, that what DCO will allow.
- You can only have one DCO ad per ad set, which becomes a problem if the previous bullet point applies to you.

Still, DCO works well so test it occasionally.

You set up DCO at the ad set level as shown below:

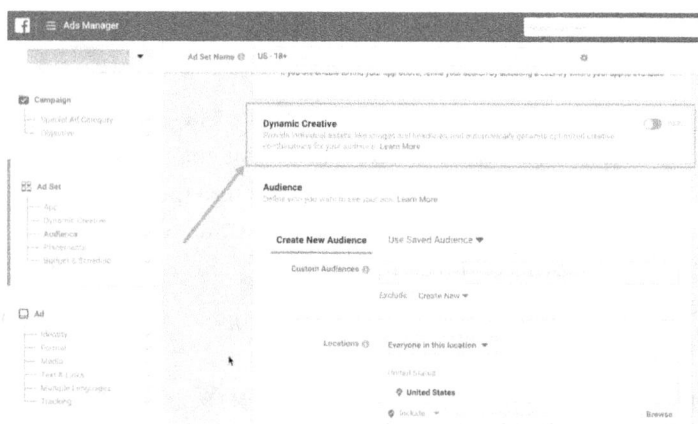

AUTOMATED RULES

Facebook's automated rules are very sophisticated, and as the name implies, they help you automatically manager your ad account. Need CPIs to stay under $6? Then automate a rule to automatically pause ad sets when they exceed $6. Want to automatically increase your budget by 30% when yesterday's ROAS is over 25%? An automated rule can help. I never use these though, because I'm so involved with the campaigns every day. I would only set such a rule temporarily when traveling, and thus cannot look at my accounts as often as I'd like. Still, you may find them helpful. More info is here: https://www.facebook.com/business/help/1694779440789213

FACEBOOK ADS MANAGER FOR EXCEL (PLUGIN)

This is a must-have tool for analyzing your data. Exporting data from Facebook is a pain because it's slow, and you must specify all the correct columns every time. The Excel Plugin makes it super fast to look at all the data you could possibly want. https://www.facebook.com/business/help/728487467327177?helpref=page_content

DYNAMIC LANGUAGE OPTIMIZATION OR DLO

If your app and app store page is localized to multiple languages you can serve ads to people who speak that language. You do this through Dynamic Language Optimization or DLO. Essentially, you create your ad in English, and then in the ad part of Ads Manager, you can add multiple languages. For example, if your serving ads in Canada but want to reach English, French, and Spanish speakers, you'd also upload your Spanish and French ad copy and ad variants, and Facebook will then detect which ad to serve which person, based on their computer settings. More info is here: https://www.facebook.com/business/help/728487467327177?helpref=page_content

Note: no need to specify a language at the ad set level. Facebook no longer needs that information, and it'll just make your ad set more expensive. The only exception is if you want to exclude English-speaking folks. Then in that case, you'd need to select all the non-English languages you want to target. Yet, at the ad level, you'll still make your English ad, and then scroll to the bottom to add the other languages as mentioned in the link I just shared.

DELIVERY INSIGHTS

This is a hidden gem that isn't super obvious, but is rich with information that will help you analyze important information about your ad set such as auction competition, audience saturation, audience overlap, etc.

You can find it here:

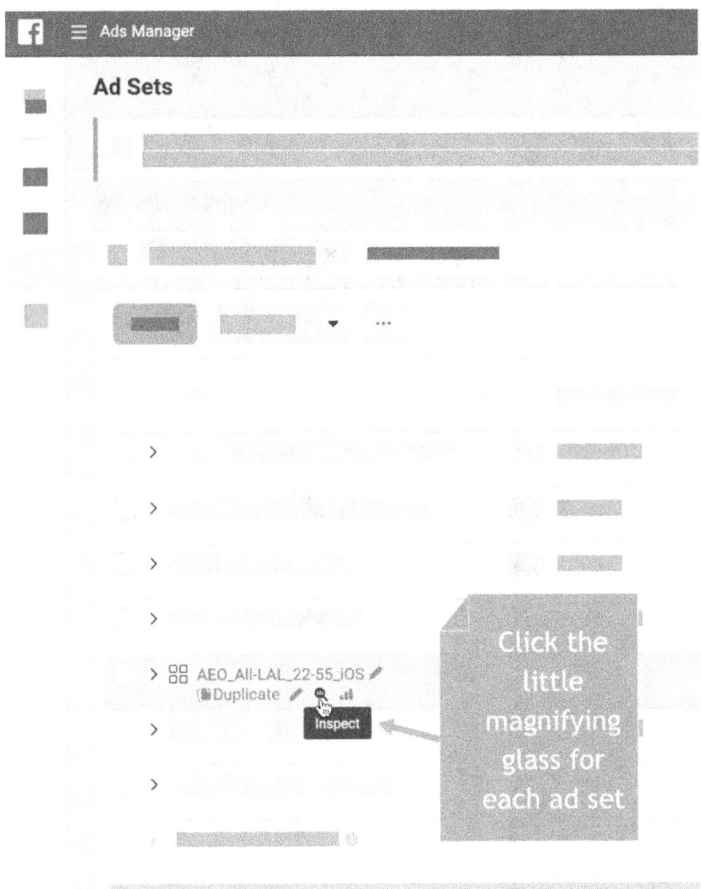

COMPETITOR ADS

Get inspiration by viewing competitors ads directly in Facebook. Head to Facebook, search for your competitor's page. Once on the page, click "See More" in the "Page Transparency" section as shown below:

78 | MICHAEL B. CASTILLE

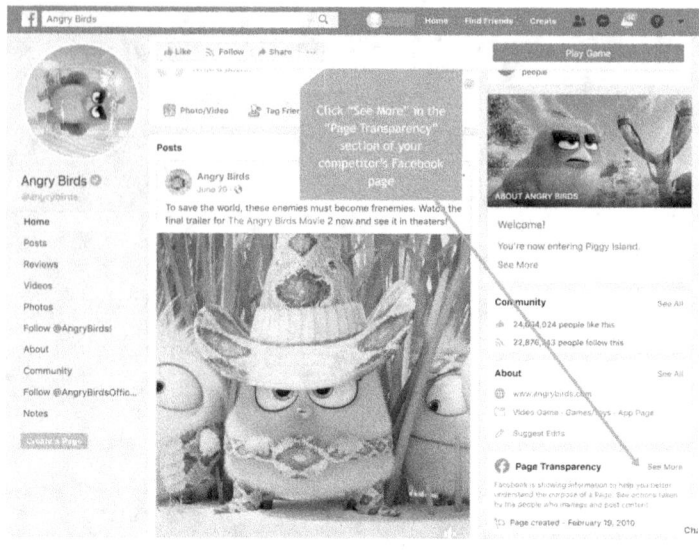

Then click "Go to Ad Library" as shown:

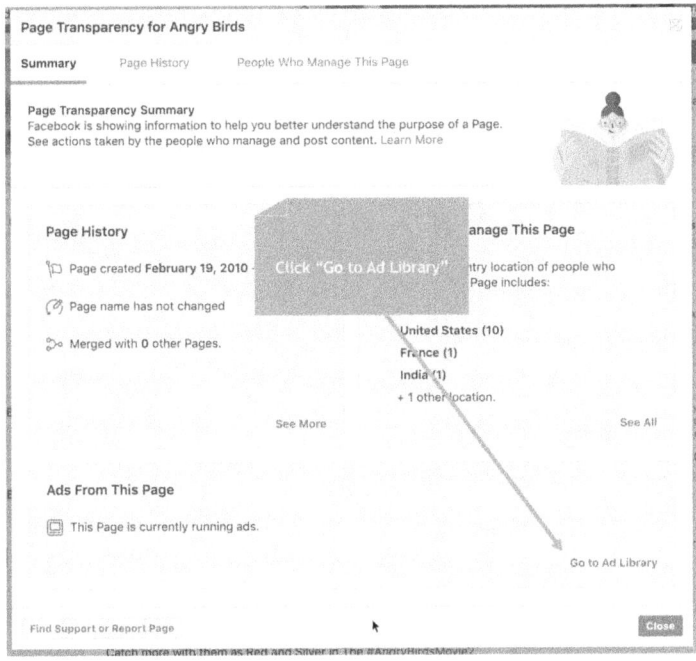

You can then review the ads they are running at the moment, as shown below:

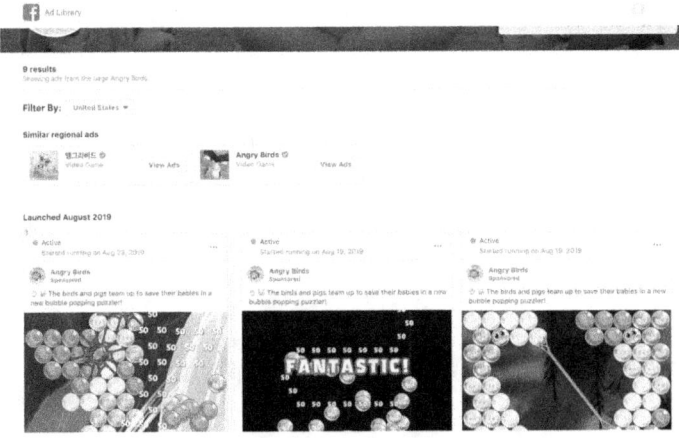

CONCLUSION

I hope this book will assist you in setting up your Facebook advertising campaigns for mobile app game marketing. I wish you the best of luck as you acquire users for your game, and of course, revenue. Happy advertising!

APPENDIX I: ADDITIONAL RESOURCES

FACEBOOK CASE STUDIES FOR GAMES

Take a look at how other games have performed on Facebook. Some of these are desktop games, but most are mobile:

https://www.facebook.com/business/success/categories/gaming

FACEBOOK INDUSTRY INSIGHTS FOR GAMES

Similar to the case studies above, this link includes both desktop and mobile, but this will provide some interesting information for you.

https://www.facebook.com/business/insights/vertical/gaming

FACEBOOK BLUEPRINT PROGRAM

Learn much more detailed information by getting certified through Facebook's Blueprint Certification program: https://www.facebook.com/business/learn/certification

Or if you want to just learn without the pressure of a cert, then check out their online courses, though keep in mind many of them are best understood in the context of web marketing rather than mobile marketing: https://www.facebook.com/business/learn/courses

INDUSTRY SOURCES

Ask questions on Quantmar which is a forum that discuss Facebook marketing for mobile apps: https://quantmar.com/

Follow Mobiledevmemo, which is a blog that shares industry knowledge and also provides advanced techniques. The guy that runs Quantmar also runs this: https://mobiledevmemo.com/

Do web searches. There's tons of info out there. If you want to know benchmark metrics, strategies, best practices, do a web search.

OTHER AD NETWORKS BEYOND FACEBOOK

At some point, you'll wonder if you should be running ads on more ad networks than just Facebook. Facebook is 99% of the time the best when it comes to driving the best ROAS. However, other good channels are Google UAC, Apple Search, and Snapchat.

APPENDIX I: ADDITIONAL RESOURCES

Check out this guide for more information.

APPENDIX II: TERMS

- **ARPU**: average revenue per user. This is simply the total revenue divided by installs for any time period.
- **ROAS**: return on ad spend. This is simply the total revenue earned from Facebook, divided by the total cost spent on Facebook. Nothing more. Don't calculate operating costs, app store fees, agency commissions or any of that.
- **COHORT**: a cohort is a group of users acquired during a particular time period. In mobile marketing, we always track the performance of cohorts. Example: let's say you acquire some users in the first week in April (April 1 - 7). You'll use AppsFlyer to continue to check how that group of folks is monetizing. Or you may want to look at monthly cohorts rather than weekly. So you'd use AppsFlyer to see how - for example - your February cohort is monetizing. You spent $10k for this group, and by June, these users have spent $20k. Not bad.
- **UA**: user acquisition. This is just a fancy way of

saying that you are advertising on Facebook (or some other network.)

- **FEATURE**: A feature is when Google Play or the Apple App Store lists or "features" your app in any sort of "best of the best" list. For example: Top games. These used to be super lucrative, but in recent years, a feature only really impacts your revenue/install volume if you receive a front-page feature, as opposed to your app feature being buried on some niche page, like best RPG games.
- **TRACKER**: A tracker is like Google Analytics for mobile apps. It tells you the performance (i.e. retention, monetization, and more) for each source, such as Facebook. It can drill down into the ad-level, letting you know how each ad is performing.
- **SOURCE**: A source is the entity that aided in acquiring the user. Facebook is a source. Snapchat is a source. Any of these paid ad networks are sources. But a source can also be organic.
- **ORGANIC**: Google Play is "organic" and the Apple App Store is "organic" because users find their way to the store naturally, without the help of ads.
- **SDK:** An SDK is block of code placed in a mobile app that allows 3rd parties to track what goes on inside the app, and even before the app. Facebook has an SDK so that it can see who has installed. AppsFlyer and other trackers have an SDK so it can attribute sources to the right ad network.

www.ingramcontent.com/pod-product-compliance
Lightning Source LLC
Chambersburg PA
CBHW070435220526
45466CB00004B/1684